另一种温情

情歌集

雪迪

Other Books by Xue Di

Flames (paradigm press, 1995. Second edition, 2000)
Translated by Keith Waldrop with Wang Ping & Iona Crook

Heart into Soil (Burning Deck & Lost Roads, 1998)
Translated by Keith Waldrop with Wang Ping, Iona Crook, Janet Tan &
Hil Anderson

Circumstances (Duration Press, 2000)
Translated by Keith Waldrop with Hil Anderson & Xue Di

An Ordinary Day (Alice James Books, 2002)
Translated by Keith Waldrop with Wang Ping, Iona Crook, Janet Tan &
Hil Anderson

Forgive (Blue Light Press, 2004)
Translated by Keith Waldrop, Forrest Gander, Sue Ellen Thompson with
Wang Ping, Hil Anderson & Waverly

ANOTHER KIND OF TENDERNESS

LOVE POEMS

BY
XUE DI

Some of these translations were first published in *Arts & Letters*, *Bomb*, *Manoa*, *Moonrabbit Review*, *The Providence Journal*, *Spectrum* and *Two Lines;* and *Heart into Soil* (Burning Deck & Lost Roads); *Circumstances* (Duration Press); *An Ordinary Day* (Alice James Books).

ISBN: 0-9723331-4-2

Cover art by Qin Feng, *Roaming Gods No. 33*, oil on canvas
Typesetting and design by E. Tracy Grinnell

Distributed by Small Press Distribution
1341 Seventh St. Berkeley, CA 94710

www.spdbooks.org

ANOTHER KIND OF TENDERNESS

LOVE POEMS

BY
Xue Di

TRANSLATED BY
Keith Waldrop
Forrest Gander
Stephen Thomas
Theodore Deppe
Sue Ellen Thompson

WITH
Hu Qian
Wang Ping
Hil Anderson
Waverly
Iona Crook

LITMUS PRESS
BROOKLYN • 2004

目录

CONTENTS

SEE HOW THE SOUL, IN THESE LOWLANDS, LOVES THE BODY

Another Kind of Tenderness is one of poetry's miracles. How else explain it? In the natural order of things, a boy who is beaten daily does not become a poet this gentle and wise; a six-year old abandoned by both parents in Beijing (a city then of about 8 million people) does not become a man who can write such a luminous book of love poems.

Miracles can begin with a book. When Xue Di was living on his own at twelve, he found a discarded volume of Pushkin's poetry. This was during the Cultural Revolution when the punishment for reading foreign books could be severe. Xue Di (pronounced shway dee) hid the book and read it secretly.

"His poetry saved my life," Xue Di has said of Pushkin. Not only did the lonely adolescent find enough hope to continue living but, "Poetry saved me from being a mean or hostile man." To write poems of such beauty, the boy reasoned, it was necessary to become a good person, capable of attentiveness, compassion, and wisdom. That sentiment might be mocked in some corners, but Chekhov would have understood, or van Gogh, or Keats.

Universities in China were closed during the Cultural Revolution, so Xue Di did not attend college. Instead, he worked for ten years in a light bulb factory. By the late 1980s, he began to feign illness so he could stay home and devote himself to his poetry. By 1989, he'd had two volumes of poems published in China. Emotional, unsparing, and wildly imaginative, these books marked Xue Di as one of the most important avant-garde poets of his generation. That summer, he helped organize writers to support the hunger strikers in Tian'anmen Square. He witnessed the tanks rolling, and after the massacre, he helped carry a wounded citizen to a hospital. By December, 1989, Brown University invited Xue Di to be a Visiting Fellow in the department of English, a position he still holds.

Another Kind of Tenderness opens with a splendid sequence of lyric poems. "Cat's Eye in a Splintered Mirror" is unmistakably contemporary yet it also feels rooted in the tradition of Li Po and Tu Fu. Like the poems of the Tang dynasty, the poet is presented as an exile, a wanderer, moving through "unfolding layers of landscape," recalling the one he loves:

> Then the lowlands. The wailing of deer
> sounds from a disappearing landscape
> I'm thinking of you. Late at night
> the return road fills with turns

Natural imagery is lush and evocative:

> When you're in love, the April coast gets
> rained on daily. While tiniest lizards crawl
> from a pool of mud, the lean long-distance traveler
> pushes his journey forward in momentary sunshine
> A fox wails amid clouds floating downwards

Xue Di knows how to allow abstractions to blend with striking particulars and how to keep his imagery fresh and modern:

> See how the soul, in these lowlands, loves
> the body—long mystery of our lives
> Now with dark, bats in a flurry
> swoop down. A yellow weasel hunts for garbage
> through an ordinary man's dream...

Poets will study this sequence, learning how to write freshly and timelessly, but more importantly, this is the sort of poem lovers will read to each other out loud:

> Classical, this face, elegantly
> sidelit. Breasts small and round
> exquisitely naked in the fine detail
> of words. A waterfall flies towards
> shallower waters, the shadow its wing
> dimming those delicate nipples

I have noted the influence of traditional Chinese poetry and of Pushkin, but Xue Di also learned from Baudelaire, and his love poetry can probe the darker aspects of the human soul as well as woo and celebrate. In "First Love," the poet finds himself

> in a hard grip
> pulled along. Wolves
> prowl in all directions

"A Man Alone" is another poem that meditates on the difficulties of love:

> Love too much or love too little:
> either way you are ridiculous, embarrassing.
> No one wants your company.
>
> Put love out of your thoughts.
> Forget it. Do.
> Try making trouble.
> Be a summer storm,
> a string of storms,
> a flood to drown the roots...

There's nothing sentimental in these poems. As the poet declares in "Love":

> In the name of
> love, you lay waste your life

But if "Love in difficulty is my / poem," there's also a generous, affirmative note in these pages and the collection ends with a series of celebratory poems, "My Home," "Saint-John Perse's 'Palm Trees'," and "The Passage to Heaven." It's a hard-won finale: we've had to accompany the lover through desolation as well as joy. But as Xue Di said in an interview with Melissa Clark:

> Poetry has to complete a procedure: first descent and then ascent. Without descent, there is no power or force in poems; without ascent, there is no spirit...and no feeling of flight.

Think of the heart as the antechamber to both Heaven and Hell. This book invites us inside and helps us explore those vast territories. By the end, we're flying. And, as a twelve-year-old once found in Beijing, lives are changed during such journeys.

– Theodore Deppe

给她

for Her

碎镜里的猫眼

Cat's Eye in a Splintered Mirror

1

沿着这条河，请求的姿式
使秋天的水精确地反映
树林的金黄。三个白天的
处子，在被说出的光芒中，
环绕第十月
托起那片带骨头的红色——
燕子向左飞翔。牛腿在变窄的
水里下沉。城市在此时
透着人情味。湿淋淋的
划船人的身体，他们向前的速度
使夜提前来临。河是两个人的开始。

向回走的人使地平线模糊。
夜鸟在断木头的反光中叫着。
长着孤独的脸的狗
正在努力穿过小树林旁
儿童游艺场那座铁门。
我的身体在激烈的紧张中
靠近你。那个夜晚
我感到你的另一种样子，
我在睡梦里向亮处走。
你头顶水罐，在红色栅栏边；
乡村少女，身后是黄土路，
土路后是闪亮的暖和的海。
当唇在加厚的时间里感觉唇，
獾结成伙，祝贺我们的爱；
马群在远处的马厩里嘶叫；
独身的航海人，黑夜里
正把细长的船驶出
静静环抱着的海湾。

1

Along the river, a stance of petition
allows autumn waters faithfully to reflect
golden yellow woods. Three blatant
virgins of day's light-rays
hover around the tenth moon
supporting that stretch of bone-like red
Swallows fly leftwards
Cows' hooves sink down in
ever narrowing waters. The town is just now
filling with human touch. Wet bodies of rowers
in their hurry to go forward, speed the coming
night. The river: two persons begin to be

One who looks back blurs the horizon
Night birds cry, reflected in broken wood
A dog with a lonely expression
tries to pass the iron gate of a
children's woodland recreation center
My body approaches yours
in a state of nerves. That night
I witnessed another you
In a dream, I was walking towards the light
You stood by a red fence, pitcher on your head
a country girl, yellow dirt road behind you
and behind the yellow dirt road a warm and glossy sea
As lips feel lips in the thick of time, badgers
gather, congratulating us on our love
Horses whinny in a stable off in the distance
In the dark of night a bachelor sailor
sails his slender boat
out of the harbor, in serene security

2

这些我喜爱的字
从红树的油里出来，带着
独身人的叹息，朝向你。
在正午兰翅鸟的瞌睡中，
一部分快乐的词紧挨着，
短小的手臂在向西的风中
优美地举着。古典的香味
隔街的马驹喷着响鼻。
孩子在抒情的单行道上奔跑。
松果在午后的光线中向下掉着。
另一些词在硬土上跳动，
肃穆地，携带短小的阴影。
灰猫在此刻，穿过客厅里
那面长镜。准确的词
寻找清静和结实的屋子。

给草坪上肥的男人离开了。
两只带黄斑点的鸟，六月
在炎热的大雨里，
在这个安宁、雅致的长廊里
造巢。圆型流动的水
是你深深爱着的样子。
长而亮的汽笛在大雾中
为返回的鱼群彻夜啸叫。
天鹅领着鸭群在你的短睡里
游动。傍晚的鸟
使暗下去的天空怀着柔情。

2

These characters I love
come towards you out of the oil of
red trees, sighing a bachelor's sighs
In a blue-winged bird's noon nap
a cheerful batch of words get into
line, their short little arms extended gracefully up
in the west wind. Classic redolence
A pony snorts across the street
Kids race a lyric one-way road
Pine nuts fall down through afternoon rays
Other words bounce on the hard ground, carrying short
shadows with them, and with what solemnity
Now a gray cat passes through a tall mirror
in the living room. Precise words
search out a quiet and a solid house

Gone is the man who manured the grassland
In June two birds with yellow speckles
fly scorching storms
to build their nest in this refined and
tranquil corridor. Such a ring of waters
images your love's depth
In heavy fog, a long loud horn
wails the night through for fish returning
A swan conducts a flock of ducks
swimming through your short slumber. Birds at dusk
fill the darkening sky with hints of tenderness

3

当你爱着，转身，雨水里的鹿
向亮处跑。山猫使阴影中的山坡
倾斜。马群背后的海
在向高处走的人的额里闪耀。
当你爱着，临海一带的四月
天天下雨。最小的蜥蜴爬出
一片泥时，削瘦的远行人
在片刻的阳光里赶路。
狐狸在移向低处的云中尖叫。

山鸡在大雾里飞的更远。
猫头鹰在来访者的背后叫着，
远处的白房子变暗。当你爱着，
我坐在朝西的倾斜的长椅上：
前面的山峰结成群
在落日的光辉中伸延，抵抗
远方那闪耀金光的海——
海水后面，是你在亲人的围绕中
大笑；是一个逐渐幸福的
善良女人诚恳的爱。

4

Stones, through hollow walls, gathering
in deserted upland. Noon wind's dizzy singsong from
a local flock. Behind the dim-faced farmer
wheat fields grow sweeter
Water flows upward through scattered roots
making the pure earth visible
to the toiler

Unexpectedly a traveler from afar
arrives at this very angle, to revisit
his perennial soul-mate. In the brief light
their given bodies address each other
See how the soul, in these lowlands, loves
the body—long mystery of our lives
Now with dark, bats in a flurry
swoop down. A yellow weasel hunts for garbage
through an ordinary man's dream. A glittering steel tower
fades in a tubercular's memory

To comprehend an enduring abstract journey
find an angle, then walk it upwards
Now: keep within pure knowing

5

想你在风景展现的层次里:
远方明亮, 近景在被强调的
暗影中。冷色的花在亮光里模糊。
靠水的人爱低处的城市,
长途旅行者, 在经验中向高处走。
事物: 以最现成的姿态出现。
红颈的黑色山鸟, 当我想起你
就飞向更远的一棵树。

更远的树更孤独。在落日中
最先暗下去。飞起的群鸟
使阴影快速向下覆盖。
观景者令远处暗下来,
然后是低处。鹿的鸣叫
从消逝的风景里传来。
我想着你。返回的路
在深夜里出现更多的转弯。

5

Imagine you're in unfolding layers of landscape
bright in the distance, a foreground of accented
shadows. Cool colored flowers in light turn hazy
A man living by the water loves lowland cities
The long-distance traveler ascends in experience
Things pose themselves as they are. When I
think of you, that mountain bird, black with a red neck, flies
towards a farther tree

The farther tree is lonelier. At sunset
it's the first to dim. Birds on the wing
hasten shadows downward
Sightseers make the distance dim
Then the lowlands. The wailing of deer
sounds from a disappearing landscape
I'm thinking of you. Late at night
the return road fills with turns

6

象征地进入人群。鸿雁
把高处的钟楼带走。
徒步的人让一座城市，向
四个方向打开。旅游者，熟知
位于好地区的街道，那儿
更少垃圾，更多狗的排泄物。
园工细腻地修理花圃，
取悦独身女人，也把时间拉长。
乌鸦在集体的孤独中瞌睡。
萨克斯风曲子在纵酒者的记忆里
尖锐地、时断时续地演奏。

你在挤得结实的人群里
坚持。向不幸福的大家族微笑。
四月的某一天雨季突然中止。
傍晚的燕子向下飞；晚安的
钟声，从河岸那边传来。
码头里铁锚成群向上升，
栈桥纷纷沉入冰凉的
水里。海湾出口处的灯塔
在落日里等待。你恰如其分地
转身，向海边那栋白色
温馨的小房子走去；
几棵在侧面的花园的树
开着花；猫在你偏爱的
灌木下面躺着。远处的落日
在从发黑的海平线上
一点一点消失。

6

Symbolically, into the crowd. The swans
have carried the bell tower down from the heights
Those on foot force a city to unfold in
four directions. Tourists know well
the streets that bound rich areas where
there is less trash, but more dog shit
The gardener trims carefully the transplants
pleasing that spinster and also stretching time out
Crows are dozing in a collective loneliness
On and off, a saxophone plays with precision
in a winebibber's memory

In a packed crowd you
keep your place, smiling at this unhappy horde
One day in April, the rainy days suddenly end
At dusk swallows fly downwards, evening
chiming from the other bank of the river
In the harbor anchors are weighed right and left
all the piers sinking in ice cold
water. The beacon at bay's outlet
waits in the sunset. Ready, you
turn and walk toward that
snug white seaside cottage
A few trees in the garden at its side
are blossoming; the cat lies under the bush
to which you are partial. The setting
sun is disappearing from
dim sea level, little
by little

7

外省变暖。中午使近处的山峰寂静。
远处白色的海水
使带风景的写作间更暗。
你在一首短诗的每个标点前停下，
文雅地，侧面的光照亮
这张古典的脸。又小又圆的
乳房，在词确定的细节里
精致地裸露；水鸟向浅水带
飞着，双翅间的阴影
使那对精巧的乳头变暗。

白天鹅抽象地静卧水中。
它们整齐展开的红蹼
使湖水里的天空更蓝，
使你柔和的腹部更平坦。
旅行者明确进入平行的
世界，在竖琴的震颤中
向深处走。然后是你
那声稍带倦意的叹息；
遥远的景色中的人，
在向下的平静阴影里站着。
钟声在模糊的十字路口
振荡— 单身的远行人
带着那张爱人的脸返回。

7

Out of state temperatures go up. Noon
makes nearby peaks
hush. White breakers in the distance obscure
a view from the study. Such a short poem to
pause before each punctuation mark
Classical, this face, elegantly
sidelit. Breasts small and round
exquisitely naked in the fine detail
of words. A waterfowl flies towards
shallower waters, the shadow of its wing
dimming those delicate nipples

White swans abstract and quiet
sitting on the water. They stretch out red feet
turning the sky in the lake even bluer
and your soft belly flatter yet
Clearly the traveler is entering
a parallel world, out into the deep
as a harp vibrates. Then comes that
sigh of yours, a sigh
of being barely tired. A man stands in the
distance, in the still downward cast of shadow
At the blurred intersection a bell begins to
ring. Returns from long journeying
a lone traveler with the face of a lover

孔雀的屏在最细的铁里
向东打开。东方是一支
金光灿灿的号，号嘴朝西。
当你修长的腿的下半部
在细微的光中展露：
12支玫瑰在爱中精致地
搭配。悠扬的号声
在过路人忧郁的姿式中
回荡。棉花田在甜味里
向前延伸。鹰不动的双翅
使远方的家园，清晰地
屹立在流放者心中。野马群
奔腾，裹着明亮的尘土，
在那些自然的、最优美的日子里！

In thin-beaten iron the tail of a peacock
spreads, facing east. East is a glittering
golden horn, its mouth towards the west
When the first faint light makes visible
the lower length of your long legs, twelve
roses in love arrange themselves
in pairs. Pedestrians stand in
gloom amid blared car-horn
melodies. Cotton fields stretch outward
sweetly. The motionless wings of an eagle
make a distant home stand out in the
mind of a man in exile. Raising bright
dust, wild horses gallop off into
those days, most ordinary, most beautiful

8

特别的字在坏天气里
让我感动，认识在远方的
那些人。壁炉里
比熟铁更有献身性的木头
燃烧，更急的一场雨
来临。飞得很慢的孤鸟
使天空越来越低。那封信
仍在我的手上。雾
正在最窄的峡谷里升起。

在越走越低的景色里，
相信另一个方向
中途的那道门仍旧打开着。
那里的鸟儿扎群，订婚的鹿
跟随返回的独身人。
落日里，急转弯处的树林
雄浑地屹立，背后
是闪亮的山峰。向上
桑塔克鲁斯山里的一棵红松
顶部闪耀着光，
整个躯干都在高处的
深刻、辽阔的黑暗里。

8

In bad weather, certain words
touch my heart, acquaint me with those people
in a faraway place. Burning in the fireplace
is wood more ready to give itself to flames
than wrought iron. A heavier rain is
coming. One solitary bird soaring slowly
forces the sky lower and lower. That letter
is still in my hand. Fog
rises through the narrowest canyon

Now I climb down the landscape
believing that in another direction
the central gate remains open
There birds flock together, betrothed deer
follow the single man returning homewards
At sunset, woods at the sharp bend
stand staunchly erect, behind them
brilliant mountain peaks. Atop
Mount Santa Cruz rises a Korean pine, its
tip glittering with light, but the entire
trunk caught in that deep and
vast darkness way up there

9

在丁字路口，下午的阳光
使正面的墙变旧。牵牛花的边缘
再一次卷曲，黑狗
朝着一栋红色的房子吠叫。
我向左转，是你
迎面跑来。女人的脸
红红的，两眼盈满
无比透彻的湖水——
雪白和青色的水鸭，
在你柔情的凝视中
成群地向上飞。20年前
京都的一个少女，
当我略感困倦时
就在一条安静的街上跑着，
耸立的乳房在夏天
薄薄的抒情的衣裳底下颤动。

深处的海水是蓝色的。
被深深爱着的，对细节
更敏感。那些小小的
金色的蟹，从落潮的海浪里
亮晶晶地爬出来。出海的船
在傍晚先后返回；
向低处去的石堤变暗。
但是前方船只入口处
那座孤塔里的汽笛，
朝着深海，仍旧
短促地，不停止地鸣叫。

9

At a T intersection, afternoon sunshine
makes the forward wall look
old. Once again a fringe of morning-glory
curls upwards. A black dog
barks at a red house. As I turn
left, it's you running
towards me. Your womanly face
rosy, your eyes filled with
water crystal clear
Ducks white and blue fly
upward in groups
within your loving gaze. In Beijing, twenty
years ago, myself listless, a young girl
ran along a quiet street, pointy breasts
bobbing under a summer
dress at once flimsy and lyric

Water in the deep sea is blue
Deeply loved, we are more sensitive
to details. Those tiny golden
crabs crawl from waves of ebb tide
glistening. Boats that have been out to sea
return in the dusk one after another
Light on the downward dyke is fading
but at the forward boat entryway
the siren from a lone tower
facing the open sea, still shrills
shortly but endlessly

10

在匀称的肉体周围的美。

闪耀的、小小的现实。
平滑地向下延伸的山谷,
白色的山羊在丝绸盖住的阴影里。
海岸地带的红尾鹰
在柔和、充满弹性的女人之间飞翔。
远处城市的灯火,跨过海水
在更远的夜空均匀地照耀。

我在回忆中颤栗。我在
被精确、鲜明地分割的现实里。
你的双乳在暗的地带
丰满地充盈。最透明的玻璃
在恒温中向里弯着。门外的海洋
不停息地在黑暗的沙子上
冲动。谈话永远、永远错开。
前一晚来访的人们坐在
平台尽头。海滩在右边
接受退去的海水。远方
三堆篝火在黑夜里燃烧。

青春和最无邪的岁月,在你
一对柔软的、小小的乳头里。
公羊的黑角在极限中向内卷着。
另一种与你的丰盈毫不相接的美,
在停止交谈的客人眼里闪耀。
海的分开的浪头,向圆型
鼓起的地带滚动。最小的山鸟
数日前飞出最小和紧的圈子。

10

Beauty outlines a body well proportioned

Glittering bit of reality. The valley stretching
smoothly down the mountain
White goats in the silken shadow beneath
A red tailed eagle of the seacoast area
glides between gentle and resilient women
Across the sea, the lamplights of a far city
radiate evenly into the night sky of beyond

I am shivering in memory. I exist
in a reality precisely and distinctively divided
Your breasts grow full and round
in the dark. The most transparent glass
concave at constant temperature. Out there
the sea throws itself repeatedly against dark
sand. No message ever gets across
Last night's visitors sit at the edge
of the patio. The beach on the right side
receives the receding tides. In the distance
three campfires in the dark of night

Youth and the years of innocence
reside in your small soft breasts
The black ram horn twists itself to the limit
Another kind of beauty, not connected to your full figure
shines in the eyes of visitors no longer talking
Sea waves, one after another, roll toward
a dome shaped area. Days ago, a little mountain bird
flew in a tight but tiny circle

阳光和欲望中，被过分
爱着的情人身体。泉水
在变甜的果子之间流动。草地
在叙述者的眼里变深。俯冲的
鹰，给挚爱着的女人，带来
一阵颤抖。异地的飞禽
在变暗的气流中尾部深红。

带高光的樱桃在男孩
向内的手指间。略小的乳房
文雅、宁静，斜斜地向上翘；
象总是深深地理解的那种爱，
在很近的距离独立存在。中间的
那堆篝火层次鲜明地燃烧；
焦木头的气味向下掉；海草
湿漉漉的，使在暗处的谈话者
脸部发亮。你恳求着，
在这样的风景中多呆一会儿。

自然的、美丽的双乳
赋予人内在的好品格。乳头
叹息，一小群鹿优雅地走进山谷。
山峦在纯粹的意境中起伏，
向远处去的落日，使近处的水景更亮；
更亮的夜晚，在清晰的层次中
完整地闪耀。海鸟
在深夜从远处飞向亮处。
我的左手，贴着优美、晶莹的弧线，
很慢地、独立地向下掉。

In sunshine and desire, a lover's body
can be loved to excess. Spring flows
between sweetening fruits. The grassland
deepens in the narrator's eyes. An eagle diving
causes the woman deep in love to shiver
for a time. A bird from somewhere else
with crimson tail in the darkening atmosphere

A glistening cherry in the boy's
bent fingers. Smaller breasts
elegant and quiet, tilting up (as love
deeply understood exists
independently) but close to each other. The campfire
between is burning up layer by layer
exuding the odor of charred wood; wet seaweed
causes the speaker's face to glow in the dark. You beg
to stay longer in such a scene

Natural and beautiful breasts
bestow on a woman her good character
Nipples sigh. Small groups of deer enter the valley
elegantly.   Mountains undulate in pure mood, the distant
setting sun brightens the nearby coastline
Brighter night as totality, shining in
distinct layers. Late at night, sea birds
fly from afar toward brightness
My left hand slowly falls on its own
along a graceful glistening curve

11

你半跪着，一头羚羊走进低谷；
晚祷的钟声从金色麦田深处

传来。熟透的是那对
下坠的果核突出的果子，

水鸟细小的脖颈湿漉漉的，
在暗处，城市的边缘

正被灯火照亮。白塔
在你急促站起时更倾斜；

灰獾尖叫，夜空显得更亮，
睡得最晚的人更幸福。

告别的夜晚，使我在
将来的日子里无所事事，

注意细节。海在最近的
深色沙丘上，雪白地震荡；

热带的密集的草从那儿消失。
观景人在雾中站立，

三个男人，吆喝号子，
沿着黑色的礁石丛向下

11

You go down on one knee, an antelope enters the valley
Deep from golden wheat fields comes the chime of

evening prayer. Fruit hang down in tandem, ripe
kernels popping

The slender neck of a water bird glistens
damp. Dark, the fringes of a city

glow with lamplight. White towers
tilt farther when you stand up suddenly

A gray badger screams, the night sky brightens
Last one to sleep is happiest

The night I take leave of leaves me
nothing to do come day

Pay attention to details. The ocean shivers snow-
whitely by a dark dune it washes

Tropical grass, once dense, is now
disappearing. Sightseers stand in fog

Three men singing a work song
plod down black rock

拖拽一条黄色木船，
另一阵更高、雪白的浪头

正在夜色中飞跃他们的头顶。
我写爱情的诗，虚度一生。

tugging a yellow wooden boat
Another taller snow-white wave

rolls over their heads in the dark
I write love poems, idling my life away

12

你在记忆的水晶体里
一层一层消失。山道在大雾中
缩短。松果在旁边的林子里

掉着，使向下的峡谷变深。
在两个现实里的人交谈；
整夜，海浪响亮和繁复地涌动，

我们之间的空间更清晰。
我们朝着各自的方向，走得更远。
无家可归者，正向火里

投入最大的木柴。夜鸟
在一条笔直的线上飞行。
无数黑色的海蟹，当我们缄默

吐着白沫，在明亮的沙子上
兴奋地爬。夜空响亮
离一只独立的手很近。

你在更深的雾里变淡，
明亮的部分消失。披着蓝布的
马，跟随带坡度的光影；

短腿的北美狼，在南边
那块巨大洼地的尽头
整夜嚎叫。我的手掌

仍旧感觉一对隆起的
结实、年轻的乳房。

12

Layer by layer you disappear into
the crystal of memory. The mountain path shrinks
in dense fog. Pine nuts falling in the nearby

wood deepen the descent into the canyon
People of two realities talk; all night long
the surge is loud and incessant

the space between us more clearly defined
We head each in his own direction, moving apart
Now a derelict throws a great hunk of

wood onto the fire. Night birds
fly a straight course. While we say
nothing, countless black sea crabs crawl eagerly

from white foam onto the
glistening sand. The night sky roars
close to a hand on its own

You are fading into deeper fog, brightest
parts gone. The horse blanketed in
blue follows the slant of shadows

Short-legged coyotes howl
all night long at the end of this vast low-lying
southward land. In the palms of my hands

remains still the feel of breasts
young, sturdy, pointed

13

为你写的诗，带着
一树白花的香气。
做客的人在香味最浓时

起身，狐狸隐入深谷。
荒置的红色马厩
在六月弯着脖颈，象你

周末在后花园里
读书的样子。旅行者
在你小睡时抵达

一座城市。模糊的瘦鸟
飞向钟楼的尖顶。
退潮的海把抒情的人

带出城市。热带的吸麻者
在最亮的落日中，幸福地
全身僵硬地凝视大海。

当你合上诗集，
这些季节性的花，香气正浓。

13

Poetry I write for you carries the
fragrance of a tree-full of white flowers
The visitor departs when the scent

is sweetest, a fox disappears from the deep valley
A discarded red barn
bending its neck in June looks like you

when you are reading in the back yard
on weekends. While you are having a
nap a traveler arrives

in the city. A blurred little bird
flies towards the bell tower pinnacle. Ebb tide
floats out of town the men demanding to

express their emotions. In a tropical sunset
drug addicts, bodies stiff, gaze merrily
towards immeasurable sea

As you close this book of poems, these seasonal
flowers send forth sweetest fragrance

14

河流的上游在缺雨的季节
变窄。独身的雄鹿
从一块石头，跳向另一块，
在对岸的晚霞里消失。
沿着田野上散乱的干草垛，
我终于到达河流的上游——
我们最初相爱的时刻。
峡谷的走向完全改变了
我们的生活。沿着水道

那些食草兽终生相爱，
并使他们漫步和冥想的地带
风景优美。那些我们艰苦地
追求的品格，祈祷的含义，
在一对浸入清水的苴角里。

在上游处，更完整地看见
你的爱是怎样曲折
不间断地滋润我的行程。
使我在诗的引领中，准确地
穿过峡路，一段一段向上；
使我在浅地崇拜植物
和那些唯美的动物的尊贵品格。
来到源头。独身的雄鹿
感激和谦逊地站在
耀眼的光芒中。

14

Upstream the river becomes narrower
in a season of drought. A single stag
leaping from rock to rock
disappears in sunset on the far side
Along haystacks scattered in the fields
I've finally reached the river's upstream
From when we first fell in love
the course of the valley has completely
changed our life. Along the water, herbivores
fall in lifelong love with one another
and turn this area where they roam and meditate
into a beautiful landscape. The character we
work hard to acquire, the meanings we pray for
all inhere in young antlers dipping into pure water

Upstream, I get a fuller view of
how your love winds, incessantly
moistening my journey's long thirst
how it enables me, with a lantern of poetry, to
cross precisely the valley path, going bit by bit
higher, how in the lowlands it bids me worship
the lofty nature of plants, the art of animals
Now I arrive at the source. A single stag
stands thankfully, modest
in a ring of light

新调子的夜曲

Nocturne on a New Theme

另一种温情

现在我就在等待了
你的柔情通过一颗草生长我
你的声音穿透尘土
你的嘴在时间深处
象一只蜜蜂悦耳地蜇刺我
现在我就在等待了
你的手如同一股河水
早已离去的母亲在对岸的丛林中
数着被天空洗亮的石头
啊，另一种温情
我的远离你的柔软皮肤的生命
我用五把钢叉刺进日子
看见时间的孔穴中
流出我的纯洁的饿渴
　　和七颗蔚蓝的星星
现在我就在等待了
你的一句话使我的欲望布满花朵
并使人脸的每一个姿式
　　　　充满温情

ANOTHER KIND OF TENDERNESS

And now I wait
Your gentleness spawned me in a blade of grass
Your voice cuts through the dust
In the hollow of time your
lips have stung me with their music

And now I wait
Your hand reaches towards me like a river running
My mother, long departed, on the other shore
counts stones that glisten washed by the sky
Yes, another kind of tenderness

My life deprived of your soft skin
with five steel prongs I poke
holes in time's daylight
and out come my pure hunger, my pure
thirst, along with seven deep blue stars
And now I wait
One sentence from you made my desire blossom
and filled all my utterance
with tenderness

归宿

那是一个不可知的世界
我站在路口眺望
　　　象清晨回忆
　　　夜晚杂乱的梦
象一个美丽女人
那张撇过一眼
就有强烈印象的脸

我一直在她后面
她雨中在裙下暴露的腿
象号角震动我的心扉
我终身不倦行走
背着灵魂沉重的包袱
用两根细细麻杆的腿
我的皮肤一片片剥落
路边一朵朵
风中开放的野蔷薇
我的心继续行走
在号音的转换中
把一粒粒红色骨头的种子
撒进千花开放的田野

我行走，向着那个模糊的世界
经过那扇慢慢打开的门
在光束照亮的尘土中
我听见母亲的声音
叫我的小名
我行走，啊！我泪流满面

RETURNING HOME

It is an unknowable place
A crossroads where I stand rooted
to the view as to a memory
of last night's tangled dream
I'm caught here, as though
hooked by the long eyes
of a striking woman
whose face, whose face . . .

I am always behind her
Below her dress, in the rain, her thighs
like a trumpet blast
blow open the valves of my heart
My whole life trudging along tirelessly
My burden, myself
supported on thin, ropey legs
My skin peeling away piece by piece
Roadside flowers, wild roses
blooming and my heart
continues to walk, called forward
by the transformative music
Red bone-seeds
scattered through a field of opened flowers

I make my way toward that dim world
toward that slowly opening door
where dust shines in spires of light
I hear my mother's voice
calling my nickname
and I keep going, keep going, tears streaming down my face

天使

女孩，跳个舞吧
  你的姿势里呈现出热带的果园，蜜蜂在你的指尖飞旋。我采集你心里的甜蜜，往日的歌唱充满生活的阴暗

女孩，跳个舞
  爱情的眼睛叫我颤栗，象我每天凝视心灵的深渊。我因为"爱"而活得筋疲力尽，在你的宝石里，看见"被爱"的光芒欣喜的发颤

女孩，舞蹈的女孩
  你的双胯是人类的摇篮，放满音乐、花朵、对罪恶一无所知的快乐的白天。你的纯洁的四肢，是诗行，使我读完它时觉得灵魂阵阵痉挛

女孩，从天堂跑出来的孩子
  我的赞美朴素直露，背叛我的誓言。可有几此我能看见这么纯粹的美的事物？有几此，我能这样无心挑选词汇，远离轻蔑；把生命巨大的喜悦，向折磨我的人类，献出

ANGEL

Girl, please dance
> In your poses a tropical orchard, honeybees flying around
> your fingertips. I harvest the honey in your heart
> song from the past full of the darkness of life

Girl, please dance
> Your eyes of love make me shiver like
> the abyss of soul I gaze into daily
> exhausted by living, because of love. In you
> diamonds, I see shock waves from the radiance of being loved

Girl, dancing girl
> Your hip is the cradle of mankind, brimming with music, flowers
> happy days of crime forgotten. Your innocent
> limbs are lines of verse which feed
> the rhythms of my soul

Girl! child running from heaven
> My allegory is plain and simple, betraying my own vows, but
> how many times have I seen such a pure and beautiful being? How
> often have I been careless in selecting words, remote from scorn
> offering to unkind mankind the immense joy of living?

第一次爱

重复你的名字
出生时被攥住
拽出来的感觉
我哭：本意是拒绝
世界不曾征询我
就获得了我
疼痛、迷惑、恐怖
念你的名字
苦难控制我
我的心，被肉体里
饥饿的狼群，撕扯

第一次爱
象一面镜子破碎
降生的痛苦
生命的痛苦
爱支配我。我有
被攥着
拽出来的感觉
狼群
正在四散开来

FIRST LOVE

Calling ceaselessly your name
in order to feel how I was caught and
plunged into birth
I cried, meaning to refuse the un-
welcoming world
Pain contains me
frightened and confused
calling your name
Nightmare clutches me
My heart is torn by hungry
wolves within my flesh

First love, like a mirror
broken. Pain
of my birth, life's
pain. Love leads me by the nose
I'm in a hard grip
pulled along. Wolves
prowl in all directions

希丽娅

看见你，长着豹眼羊身的孩子
在夏天切开的宝石中间
笑着。身子前倾
正午的茸茸绿草里
藏着二只正欲蹦起的蚂蚱
夏天这样扁圆地
展开。一个女孩子
用兽眼看成年人的世界
谛的世界，就象一滴
顺风的羊泪。我的
希丽娅，念你的名字
我感到罪孽深重
感到爱，纯粹的爱
凉凉的，逼迫我
嘲笑我。因为
我几乎神经错乱
凭着记忆歌唱
凭着记忆，鉴赏美
想到你，想想
你小小的年纪
为我几近四十的岁数
仍旧苦苦写诗
为了一个字，掉一撮头发
一个句子，使我暗中流泪
心情沮丧。想想
就感到羞愧
而你就是：那个
我苦苦挣扎想写出的

CELIA

I see you, with your panther eyes and the body of a lamb
among the cut gems of summer
laughing. Your body leaning forward
in the lush, sunlit grass
hiding two locusts whose only desire is to leap
Summer spreads its palm
over the land. A child
sees the sediment of the adult world
reflected in the tear from an animal's eye. My
Celia: when I speak your name
I feel sinfully guilty
I feel love, so pure
and cool it is like
laughter washing over me
My nerves are so frayed
they can only sing remembered songs
relying on memory's keen palate
I think of how young you are
compared to my nearly forty years
I still write whole poems
for the sake of a single word, sacrificing a tuft of hair
for each line, my tears flowing in the dark
Then the shame
of my effort, knowing that you
are my subject

一个豹眼羊身的孩子
在九三年的夏季，象鹿
惊慌地跑过。到处
都是凶杀的新闻
到处是性。诗人
耻于告诉别人，他写诗
麦克杰克逊被丑闻威胁
他是我喜欢的摇滚歌手
我说的是心灵
我在心情沮丧的夜晚
想到心灵。因为夏天
正在缓缓地合上
他的宝石。唉，希丽娅

A child with panther eyes and the body of a lamb
In the summer of 1993, running
like a startled deer. The news is rife
with murder and sex. A poet
who is ashamed to say he writes poems
a rock star threatened by scandal
What I'm talking about is
spirit. On a night like this, downcast
I think of spirit. Because summer
is closing its hand around me
I think of my gem, my Celia

毒品

当我在新英格兰的夏天
清晨醒来。回忆那个姑娘
她的两只乳房在我梦中
我双手仍旧残留
抓住地铁车厢里圆型把手的感觉
我不动。生命在前进
她的两只眼睛使我想起猫头鹰
我的爱在黑夜里
在荒草丛生的田野潜行
猫头鹰无声俯冲
她的嘴含着我的舌头
两只长着绒毛的长腿
夹住我的瞬间的爱
无限恐怖的喊叫

这是我每天吮吸的毒品
我爱一个女人
她的四肢白晰
她优美、文雅
她的手指轻轻
摩擦我的皮肤
爱情最坚定时
恶梦呈现
回忆左右抽打我的脸
把我推向七个方向
拼在一起。我在
不间段的暴力的梦中
在汗水涔涔的床上
爱着。爱着,干着使心灵愉悦
肉体疲倦、困惑的苦活儿
爱着,发现自己上了瘾

DRUG

Waking one summer
morning in New England, I
remembered the breasts of the girl in my dream
My hands still with the feel
of clutching the round subway strap
I stand still. Life moves on
Her eyes remind me of an owl
In the darkness, my love for her
crawls quietly through weed-filled fields
The owl dives noiselessly
Her mouth holds my tongue
Long hairy legs clamp
tight—my cry of horror
explodes in the moment of love

This is the drug I imbibe each day
a woman I love madly
Her skin is whiter than mine
She has grace, elegance. Her
fingers caress my
skin always with tenderness
But nightmares come
when love is deepest
Their memory whips my face
pushes me seven different directions
then pieces me back together
and sends me loving
in the constant, violent dreams
of my sweaty bed
Loving, hard work which
rejoices my spirit, tires and confuses my
body—I realize I'm addicted

这是新英格兰的夏天
暴力、爱、恐怖。我张开嘴
习惯舔食语言的舌头
舔食小小的乳房
毒品和诗歌搀和
流动、沸腾在我的身体
七个灵性的部位
我向前进。生命不移动
我爱那个女人。她优美、文雅
教导我放弃诗歌
在她的美丽的肉中
在我的疲惫和迷失里
在绝望的孤独和她
充满恐惧和神经质的爱中
看清，骤然明白
我——和我深深瘾上的
各是什么东西

Such is life in the New England summer
Violence, love, terror. When I open my mouth
my tongue, that's used to tasting words
tastes a pair of small breasts
I feel poetry and the drug
all mixed together. They
boil and bubble in
the seven celestial areas of my body
I move on—my life stands still. I
love that woman, such grace, such elegance
She teaches me to give up poetry
She teaches me, in her flesh, in my
fatigue and loss, in such
desperate loneliness and
in her love full of terror and hysteria
suddenly to see and to understand
the truth of myself and also
of the thing I'm so deeply addicted to

新调子的夜曲

一码，一码，朝向西方
我们开着'爱情'
时髦的车子。车头
切开白人的欢呼、失望
爱切开我们的身子
我们生活在陌生的国度
白人和亚洲人的爱
是一道烹制复杂的汤
唯一的不同是，白人
喝汤开胃。黄种人
喝汤意味
宴席结束

做爱，恨喃喃的分手
白人喜欢择直嗓子
叫喊。皮肤黄晰的人
只是一个眼神。一码，一码
在肉里移动。唯独在床上
人类被允许
尽情发泄仇恨
嘶咬、辱骂、喷吐脏话
全是爱的有味道的证明

朝向西方，我们的爱
带着慢撒气的四个轱辘
每个深夜，穿过
成长的痛苦。象一根
被打弯了的钉子
我们做爱。做出的爱
奋力穿过种族
与种族的宽阔的镂隙
那是在黑暗里
完成的过程
肉体闪耀。我们知道
我们是谁。不知
　　　我们在哪里

Nocturne on a New Theme

One after another, westward
we drive "love"—this
fashionable car. Its bumper
cuts through cheers and catcalls
Love cuts open our bodies. We
live in a strange country
Love between white and Asian
is a complicated
soup. N.B.: the white
drink soup as an appetizer
while to the Asian, soup means
end of banquet

To make love or to leave
whites like to shout at the
top of their lungs. The yellow
manage with a look. One after another
moving in the flesh. Only in bed
are humans allowed to air their
hate without reserve. Biting
cursing, backbiting—all
indicate succulent loving

Westward our love moves, on
four tires with a slow leak
Every night through the
pain of growth. Like a whacked nail
bent, we're making love. The love we've
made breaks through the gulf between
races—a work completed
in the dark. The flesh
shines. We know
who we are. Where
are we

旋

总有一天，你会衰老
你生命的车栏已褪色枯朽
你在田野上孤零地散步
手中的花朵滴入疲倦的泪珠

那时，你会想起我吗
一颗被你的轮声擦伤的
沉默的树。你会站在树前
靠着它短暂的休息
而它遍痂的身体也老态龙钟

伸出手，摘一片叶子
犹如从架子上取一部诗集
看着叶脉的横纵网纹
悄声叹息。红胸脯的鸟
拍响着翅膀远去

SPINNING

It will certainly come, your day of aging
The guard-rail of your life is already rusted and rotting
You will walk the fields alone
flower petals in your hand melting to tired tears

Then, will you think of me
A silent tree scraped by the
sound of your wheels. You will
stand by the tree, lean on it for momentary respite
its body also scarred and decrepit

reach out a hand, pick a leaf
as if taking a book of poetry from the shelf
look at the veins in their cross-hatchings
sigh quietly. A red-breasted bird
beats its wings into the distance

旋 · 2

我真想把你，用橡皮
从我的记忆中擦掉
象关上那扇悄声打开的门
可你的影子犹如墙上的表针
总是在我心中走动
我真想把你，用弓
从我的记忆中射走
象挥臂赶去停息一地的鸽群
可我又迈开布满伤痕的腿
　　四处去把你寻找
痴恋的人是不幸的人
捧着自己的心，象一颗苦涩的果子
脸色焦黄的把它咬着，吞进
如今，我再也不试图，去把
密集的悲伤驱赶。它好似蚁群
沿着鼻梁的道路向脸蜂拥
就让我孤寂地坐在角落里，一动不动
让那团柔软、尖细的哀伤
那一片摇晃的钟声，把我织住

SPINNING 2

How I wish I could blot you
from my memory
close a secret door on you
but your shadow ticks in my heart
like the hands of a wall-clock
How I wish I could aim your arrow
away from my memory
or scatter you like a flock of pigeons
but I keep on, worn out, limping
    looking everywhere for you
The lover is doomed to hold out
his heart like a green fruit, to bite
into its tartness, mouth puckered, to swallow
These days I no longer try to evacuate
my grief. It swarms me
like ants blackening my face
I'll sit, without moving, in the corner
I'll let the muted iron sadness
of a swinging bell toll for me

独自一人

这就是我们的爱
你不转身，向来的方向走
树木在春天
生长的方向朝向树根
风从树的前面吹过来
春天，人类和植物
开始发情。春天
所有的思想朝向
来的方向。这是我们的爱
当成双的手触摸到根茎
爱情在发冷。动物
四肢在对夏天
恐怖的回忆中伸缩
我在苦苦地写着
尽量什么都不想
当一节诗完成
我能感到，下一节诗
必定带着屈辱
痛苦的经验
在一开始的尝试中
猛然展现开来

这就是，爱的太多的爱
没有情，只有思想
象一个女人，乳房坚挺
面孔削瘦。她说爱你
就意味爱你。把你
像肉肠似的包起来
你感到，在爱的方式中
去掉动物的愿望
人类如此容易
感到绝望。你是一块肉
或者，剔得乾净极了的

A MAN ALONE

Our love is this:
you have not turned, and yet
you're heading backward, whence you came.
The trees in spring grow down into their roots.
Both men and plants in spring go into heat.
In spring each thought becomes original.
Our love is this:
as hands and roots make contact,
trembling comes. The limbs of animals withdraw,
as though the muscles could recall the summer's dread.
I write. I write deliberately.
I try to think of nothing as I write.
And still I feel, when I have finished one,
the stanza I go on to pained,
humiliated and provisional,
a mere experiment.

It's this: the love of love has gotten out of hand.
No feeling's left, just thoughts,
imagination: there's a thin cheeked woman
with firm breasts, who's said
she loves you. What she meant
was merely that: she loves you.
You want her to surround you
like a sausage.
It's altogether animal, this drive,
although you call it love, and yet
without it, plain despair appears.
You are a piece of meat or a clean bone.

一根骨头。你喜欢的爱
总在没有获得的部份里
爱的太少，爱的太多
都使你成为—可笑的
使人不舒服的人

干脆不要谈爱
不要去想。让你
试着在生活中犯犯混
夏天暴雨连绵
阴晦的天气伤害
事物的根茎。冬天
我们习惯坐在家里
写诗。由于百无聊赖
修改过去的作品

The love you most desire
is always where you haven't gotten yet.
Love too much or love too little:
either way you are ridiculous, embarrassing.
No one wants your company.

Put love out of your thoughts.
Forget it. Do.
Try making trouble.
Be a summer storm,
a string of storms,
a flood to drown the roots.
In winter then we'll sit at home
as usual and write our poems.
Bored, we'll fiddle with the tired lines.

巫女

生命是好玩的戏法
我把左手藏进马眼
我站在树旁；踩住的根
从舌底长出。梦里

这样被生活踩着
被单喊叫。你的
结满野草莓的手臂
环绕垫着太阳的腰

我的牙齿敲打果核
你，小小田野的巫女
用九只鹿敏捷的奔跑
眼窝伸出细细的茸角

看哪！你的指头刺着葫芦
落满花瓣的指甲
掐住我在干躁的空气中
那么颓废的肉

生命在你胯里多么美妙
你喜欢在黑夜上跳着跑
喜欢黄昏在一张兽皮上
留下骑过的痕迹

哦，小小石榴的巫女
你喜欢世界，在水珠连续
上升的欢呼里，在一颗颗
饱含汁液的坚硬的籽粒里

有着无限的清晰的痛苦吗

WITCH

Living is magical
You tuck your left hand into a horse's eye
Beside the tree I stand. Crushed roots
crawl from under my tongue. Dreams

of this kind—life tramples them
a sheet shouts. Your arms
are tied with wild strawberry vines
around the sun's soft waist

I bite into the stone of a fruit
You, diminutive backwoods witch
you run like nine deer
From your eye sockets, thin young
antlers are branching

Look! Your fingertips stab into a gourd
Your fingernails drop like petals
onto my weary flesh, pinching me

But how splendid it is at your hips
when you leap away into dark nights
and, like dusk, leave the trace of your grip
on the pelts of wild animals

Oh, small pomegranate, my little witch
Do you love the world raising its shouts
from a drop of water, from hard
tiny seeds ripe with juice?

Do you love its vivid, infinite suffering?

向内，向内

当有一天我发现
我的爱是我的
活着的疾病。病根
是我的童年
象过早播下的种子
心是好的，种子
无法穿过严寒
和在孤独里
被毁掉的童年
当我尝试着爱
我发现．实际上
我在恨。没有什么
值得怕了
除了爱、恨本身

问题不是活着还是
去死。向哪个方向走
都把疾病延伸
只是意识和不意识的问题
如果我没有试着爱
情况会好一些
我不会象现在这样
痛恨自己。抽自己嘴巴
清楚地看见
生命的有病的状态

白天，看见这张脸
越来越丑陋、衰老
看见恨，怎样在肉里
把根粗鲁地向下伸
我假装神采奕奕地活着
活的那么恶心

Turn Inward, Inward

I discovered one day that
love is my life's
disease, rooted
in my childhood like
seeds sown too early. Well
intended, but seeds can't
penetrate frost and
ruined lonely
childhood. When I
try to love, I find I'm
hating. There's nothing
worth our fear but love, but
hatred itself

The question isn't to be or
not to be. Wherever we go we
spread our disease. It's a question
of being conscious or unconscious
If I hadn't tried to love, things
would be better and I wouldn't
hate myself like this
I slap my own face and
see clearly the
sickness of living

Daylong I see this face
aging, ever
uglier. I see hatred, how its root
digs into the flesh. I pretend
to glow with health, my very

在睡眠中，全身上下
沾满了屎。睡眠
象一个粪坑。我的身体
是横在粪坑上的
一块板子。醒来
是在板子上走过去
看着脚下的粪便
奋力地爬着的肉虫
相信看见了前生
看见：内在的自我的形状

我对不起我娘的
子宫。那是比粪坑美好
温暖的地方。那里不曾
接受过爱。只是一张板子
横过去。这就是我的病根
爱人的下身，曾是我
唯一爱过崇敬的地方
唯一在那里
我让我的生命
小心翼翼经过
满含敬畏。我恨
她的头脑她的思想

我爱她两眼发亮
全身充满爱情，叫
 '操我' 的样子
我的身体充满灵感
感到此生垂直竖立
向上：在仇恨中爱
在爱里仇恨
带着成年变硬的身子
返回童年。或者
我是梦。现实生活
是我熟悉的：粪坑

life an illness. When I
sleep my covers are
shit. Sleep is a
latrine, my body
a plank across it. Waking
is to walk that plank, watching
the filth beneath my feet, the
worms at work. I think I
see my former life
I see my inward shape

I shame my mother's
womb, brighter and warmer
than this cess-pit. Love
never came there. Now there's
only a plank across. Here
is the root of my disease
My love's lower
part is all I
love and worship. Only there
I let my life
pass by with care and
in awe. I hate her
brain, her thought

I love her shining eyes
her body full of love, the way
she calls out *Fuck me*! My body
fills with inspiration
I feel this life
erect, loving in
hate, hating in love, the
hard adult body in a re-
turn to childhood. Or else I'm
just a dream. Real
life I recognize: the latrine

有一天我发现——
被爱使人堕落
爱，使人绝望

One day I discovered that being
loved makes love
dissipate, makes us desperate

晕眩

你的身体是一棵树
根纠缠着
向深处裂开的伤口
我的手掌缓缓移动
相遇是一次砍伐
你的脸是截开的树身
暴露着静静的年轮
纹路之间空白的痛苦
叹息是一群鸟
在年龄的分岔处
筑巢。你的眼睛
　那条裂缝
深处盘卷着虫子
它使我的心
一次次从暗中注视你
　时，颤抖

DIZZY

Your body, a tree
its roots tangled
in the raw center of an open wound
My palms move tentatively
When we meet, it is a felling
Your face lights up like a fresh wedge
of tree exposing the rings around your eyes
agonies recorded in the blanks between lines
Your sigh is a flock of birds
nesting in the branches of your
youth. Your eyes
are like insects curled
into fissures
In my heart's
darkness I gaze at you time and time
again, trembling

重复

活在紧张和美丽的
当地人的爱中

迷路者的脚
在一堵旧墙里走

冬天的花园，使
独居人在睡眠中消瘦

心是一间空的作坊
当小镇里唯一的河

挤满生病的恋人
雪里的太阳象减肥者

一天中最爱的芒果
记忆也在怨愤中卡住了

背井离乡人看海
怀念中死鱼成群，紧紧

抱住。时间的一副内脏
在异地衰老、烂掉的过程

连诗也在毫无想象的生活中
返回黑暗。象此地

消费以外的尘土
冬天的湖，当地人

REPETITION

Living in the love of a local woman
intense and beautiful

Lost feet
walking an old wall

Winter's garden
slimming him while he sleeps alone

The heart is an empty place to work
A small town's only river

sick lovers crowding in. Sun on
snow seems like weight being lost

Mango, the day's delight
Discontent wedges the memory

A man forced to leave his home gazes
seaward, longs for a school of dead fish held

fast. Time's inner organs
degenerate in a foreign land, decay

In a life without imagination even poetry
grows dark again. Like this land

dusty beyond consumption
Winter's lake, lake the locals

指给外来者看的湖
爱恋的人表情平静

他们密密麻麻
在明亮的冰中

point out to outsiders
Lovers expressing calm

many and together
on the bright ice

译文

看云，看见收拾花园的
独身人，把三股水
放在种子和乳牛之间

回忆童年，看见那口
倒塌的井。8只全身
漆黑的鸟，栖止

在搬到靠海的地带住的
那人的思维方式中
梦想的独居的人

抬头望日，看见孤单的
闪耀的翅膀，黑暗的
飞翔姿式。是在另一个城市

爱人心疼地说：爱
她的优雅的、匀称裸体
在我的孤独、淫秽的想象中

做白日梦的人，信仰
想象的生活
爱三股水中的花园

被童年的一次事件
持续地摧毁
黑鸟以他们各自的方式

在信命的人的梦想里
　　　　　　飞翔

96

TRANSLATION

Staring at the clouds, I see a single figure
arranging a flower garden. She sets three
streams between her seeds and the dairy cattle

Recalling childhood, I see a collapsed
well, eight full-bellied
pitch-black birds perched

among the ways of thought of
one who has moved into a strip of land
near the ocean. The man lives alone, dreaming

Lifting my gaze toward the sun, I see
a single shining wing, darkness
circling in the air. It is some other city

My loving heart in pain cries, Do love
her elegant, well-made naked body
my lonely unclean imagination

Daydream. Faith
Imaginary life
Love's flower bed beside three streams

Shattered continually by one
act from childhood
Each blackbird on its own

hovering
in the dreams of a believer in luck

内部的联系

命名在最白的雪里。
活的形式酷似
冬天的风景。蓝色的马群,

集体弯曲着脖子
在雪里熟睡。
剥芭蕉皮的孩子,

一生长得精瘦,
充满灵性、善意的孩子,
黑暗在好看的、匀称的

四肢里舞蹈。被撕开,
象在光的中心呈现的
全裸的性。和善心

美丽、湿润的女人一起,
向回卷的火。黄鼬结伙
在紧缩的野地里尖锐地叫着。

她的脸闪耀。黑夜
最小的、通灵的孩子,
独自一人时最不和谐的。

日出前返回的山鸡回忆,
野狗在小镇的暴风雪中
出没。叫雪的孤独极的

孩子,终日幻想。
在一年最暴力的一场大雪后,
看见幸福晶莹、分裂的形状。

INTERNAL RELATIONS

Christened in whitest snow
A lifestyle the very image of
winter landscape. The horses, blue

crook their necks, sleep
soundly in the snow.
The child peels Chinese bananas

develops very thin life-
long, filled with spirit and good will
Darkness dances in his fine

symmetrical limbs. Riven, like
sex emerging naked in a core
of light. Together with a

pretty woman, kindhearted, moist, the fire
surges up again. Yellow weasels gang up
screaming in a no-man's-land

Her face is radiant. Black night's
youngest psychic child
dissonant most when alone

Pheasants return in memory before sunset
Wild dogs traipse the snow in the
small town. The child called Xue

utterly lonely, fantasizes all day long
He has seen happiness, translucent, shining, shattered
heaviest snow of the year

情人节

没被爱过的童年
使一生携带疾病

早餐的饮水带着病毒
牛奶与芥末使异乡人泻肚

酒在孤独的时刻发亮
一群在湿沙子里

向远处爬的蟹
强烈地渴望得到爱

在坚决和粗暴的黑暗中
感觉爱，批评爱

病中的人，细腻地领会
病的滋味。相爱的人

带来一场暴风雪
谋生的意志丧送的

数十个年头：病毒攻心
叫死劲写诗的年头

为爱、为理解活
孤傲、伤神的青年

根在童年折断
生病的，过份追求幸福的人

VALENTINE'S DAY

A loveless childhood
makes a man contagious all his life.

His drinking water is contaminated.
Foreign milk and mustard give him shits.

A lonely cocktail gleams at him,
as pilgrim crabs across the tide flats

troop toward something too far off to see.
Fever reaches for a glass of love.

The darkness lasts and lasts
in which we get to know love with our fingertips.

We become the connoisseurs
of illness and, as lovers,

we have blizzards in our hearts.
Ambition kills us slowly.

The illness creeps from body
into mind. Its symptom is this itch

to write these poems, poems
of love, of life, of that proud,

high-strung youth, who first became detached,
and went too far in search of happiness.

甜的爵士

小心地爱。爱你
生病的肉里的一枚琥珀
东方的瓷器。公山羊的双角
在我爱时下垂，然后弯曲
离我们的爱最近的海洋:
那些盐，整齐地进入一只
狗眼。那些曾被深深爱过
迷路的眼睛

那些火，河流在傍晚
把他们带走。马群消逝
东方的夜桌。当腰与腰
象两座湖紧紧挨着
唇如鱼，游向湖底
离我们的爱最近的村庄:
所有的马驹从睡梦中
快乐地醒来

SWEET JAZZ

Love with care. Loving you
amber in sick flesh
east of China. When I love, a
pair of goat horns seems more
crooked. Our love's closest ocean's
salt flows into the
one dog's eye. Those labyrinthine
eyes once deeply loved

Those fires—the river at nightfall
carries them away. Horses vanish
night owl of the east. When torso and torso
like two lakes flow together, lips like
fish on a dive to the lake's bottom
Our love's closest village
all the ponies jolted from their dreams
                              to happy waking

意大利餐馆

多年后，那些词在你的花园里
被斜射的光打开。音调的含义，
我们什么也不说。玫瑰的叶子
在伤心的爱中安静地展开。
那些曾与我毫无关系的图片
被你柔和极的指尖捏着。
多年前我梦见鲜艳的美
和一只长腿的狍子。我们眼睛里
整只乐队在演奏。心是在旋律里的
作曲家。当手和手分开
灵魂成为挚友。星光和水中
两颗心经历的孤独。唇寻找唇，
穿过肉体和肉体的宽阔空隙。

多年后，我们在那只猫的眼里
看见深深的感激。

Paradise Restaurant

Years later, words visible by slant light
in your garden. A sense of accent, we said
nothing. Rose leaves unfold peacefully as you grieve
Between gentlest fingers you hold
photos not of me
Years ago I dreamt of brilliant beauty
and a long-legged roe deer. Inside our eyes
a whole band plays. The heart
composes melodies. When hands part
souls become intimate
Hearts alone in moonlight and water
lip seeks lip across the gap between bodies

Years later, we read grace
deep within the cat's eye

爱情的皮

在孤独中学习爱
感觉憎恨，是一颗
掉在黑暗外面的核
核的两端，是生和死
当我们感觉喜悦
我们停止询问。我们
称那样的状态为爱

从黑暗的底层，往上活
接近无知。哭泣
没有—在意识里的理由
我们把那样的状态
叫做觉醒。象一座桥
从一道深渊到另一道
深渊，从空到空
实体就是活时
每一时刻的努力
爱情裂开，看见
另一个爱情生长
感觉爱一个人的困惑
从死亡到死亡
中间只有一盏灯

在孤独中爱
一种绝望的努力
一种疲倦的活法
当我远离祖国
只在梦中返回
祖国对于我
是一层光线

THE SKIN OF LOVE

To learn to love in
loneliness and to feel
hatred is a root sunk the
other side of darkness. On
either side is life and death
When we're happy, we
stop questioning
and we call that state *love*

From the bottom of the dark, to
live upwards, approaching
unknowing. To weep. Consciousness
void of reason. That state
we call *waking*. Like a
bridge from abyss to abyss, from
void to void, the gist is
all our effort every
moment of our lives. A love
falters, see: another love grows
Love in confusion. Between
death and death there is
one lamp and one only

To love in loneliness
desperate effort
exhausting way of life
far from my own country, returning
only in dreams
Country means to me
a plane of light

是一种：被迫的
我由衷接受的活法
返回的欲望，是一块
正在变硬的皮
皮的两边
是在努力中
对生与活
死和亡的认知

a way of living I
must, and heartily, accept
The return of desire is
a calloused skin, both
sides of which strive
to know life, living
and death, dying

爱

你是否能在忘记中
学会爱。在放松中
理解爱，与自己所要的
当身体象雨里的雪地
被踩过的痕迹
即使在寒冷中
也在迅速消失
你是否能在压制着的愤怒中
理解愤怒。他们来自爱
以爱的名义和胆量
毁掉爱情。当心灵
比肉体更渴望互相接触
那是最危险的时候

绝望的时候。爱成为具体的
比性器更具体、更危险
爱是一支发狂的军队
在耻辱中的童年。爱是
你想要的一切。今生今世
你得不到的一切，向爱索要
你意识到的一切，都是
危险的。你知道开始
不知道怎么停止
以爱的名义，你滥用此生

爱是心灵的能量，是在内的
当你把他如数向外放出
他可能成为恨，并
使你失去自己。当肉体
比心灵更渴望互相接触
那是看得见出口的黑暗

LOVE

Can't you learn love
through forgetting, understand love
by relaxing. That's what you need
when the body looks like rained-on snow
as footprints
run away in haste
even while it's winter
Can you understand the rage
of repressed anger—it comes from love
and, in love's name and the name of
courage, it ruins love. When the heart
is more eager for intimacy than the body
the most dangerous moment has arrived

Desperate moment. Love becomes more concrete
than genitals—and more dangerous
Love is an army gone loco, a child
sunk in humiliation. Love is
everything you ever want, everything you
can't get in this life. You ask from love every-
thing you know anything about and it's all
dangerous. You know how to begin
but not how to stop. In the name of
love, you lay waste your life

Love is the soul's inner energy. If un-
stopped altogether, it may become
hate, and then you're lost. As long as body
is more eager for intimacy than is heart, it's
dark but you can see the exit sign

强烈的爱和强烈渴望
得到爱，是在高处的
黑暗中。那里我们学习
痛苦的、在不公平的
感觉中，度过此生

你，你和我们
爱只是灵魂的成长的开始
他也许需要几次肉体的
毁灭。肉体的极度苦难
不是灵魂的，是意识的
受难。谁懂了
谁就在高处的黑暗中
看见在高处的
　　　　　　出口

Long love and strong desire
win love. Then standing
high in the dark.   From there one can trace
the course of our lives, marked
by pain and injustice

                You. You, and
we also. Love is just the beginning of
soul's maturing. Soul may need several
bodily destructions. Body's torment
doesn't become soul's, but remains in the body's
suffering. Who understands this
stands high in the dark and
can see the exit
                up there

三月

三月即将消逝。象
越走越远的人，走的越远
越对此生充满悔意
我们在白天哭泣
为了一批告别的人群
挨的太近的肉体的空房子
震颤着，灵魂在里面号叫
灵魂要求他们的硬壳
彼此看清距离。夜晚
敏感的人写作，保持沉默
困惑的人们做爱，竭力
感觉身体之外的东西
而你整夜哭泣，肉体的
大房子空空的，回声
显得格外凄楚。我爱你
女人：在雨加雪的三月
你越走越远。对肉身
平安和稳妥的想象
使你在今生
和灵魂拉开距离

我尽量不使用身子
在崇敬的感觉中
体验成长的灵魂
和越用越老的肉体的
关系。象我在写作时
和我的许多前生交谈
在做爱时失去意识的
旅行在爱中，当肉体
感到疲惫，就感到：
返回时的闪耀和困惑
就知道怎样哭，喊叫
抱怨；和迷失的女人

MARCH

March fades. Like
a traveler, the farther he goes
the more he regrets his life
We weep day long
for the crowd on their way
Too close, empty rooms of flesh
tremble, souls howl within
demanding hard shells
for keeping their distance. At night
sensitive people write, without speaking
Confused people make love, working hard
to feel something outside their bodies
But you, you weep all night, cavernous room
of empty flesh. Rueful
echoes. Woman, I
love you. In the wet snow of March
you walk farther and farther, imagining
safety and security for the flesh
In this life, keep some distance
between you and your soul

If I could only not use my body
In the feeling of worship to
experience the soul's growing
its interaction with the
aging body. As when I write, I
talk with my many past lives
unconscious love-travel, making
love. When the body's
tired, I feel its glow
embarrassed in return. I
know how to cry, to shout
to complain. With the woman lost

一起穿过暴力的情爱
三月消逝。灵魂的喊叫
给这个拥挤的、越来
越脏的星球
带来数不尽的翻滚的风暴

we cross the fury of love
March fades. Souls crying
bring unnumbered storms
rolling to this over-
crowded dirtying
planet

困难中的爱

和解的时候
我感到接近源头
我被诗歌长长的篮子
摇着。我的手在另一个现实里
写出散发植物香气的诗句
我的肉体在困难的时刻
享受那些诗句，使在
意识中的此生获得拯救
接近源头。那是
不带有自我强烈意识的
喜悦。生命是液体
摇晃着，传送出美妙的
自在进行着的赞美
那时诗歌的篮子
就在这片明净的摇荡的
水中，上上下下
活着的人们感到爱和被爱：
清澈宁静的幸福

在困难中的爱，是我的诗
在另一个现实完整的一节
结束。新的一节诞生
还未显现出来。我摸索
返回时迷失。感到生命
在内在的自我中哭喊
感到写出第一句，就
和整个生命连接起来的艰难
此生的艰难，使此生
在另一个现实中
无阻碍地滑动。越多的爱

LOVE IN DIFFICULTY

Reconciled
I feel close to the source
I am rocked in the long ark of
poetry. In another reality my hand
writes lines with the odor of plants
My body, in its difficult
times, enjoys them—keeping life
aware and
closer to the source. Pleasure without
self-consciousness. Life is a trembling
liquid, sending out strains of
unprompted praise
The ark of poetry
glides away and along
on this clear rippling
water
People love and feel loved, feel
happiness calm and pure

Love in difficulty is my
poem. One stanza is complete. In another
reality, a new stanza is being
born, but isn't yet there
I grope for lost arrivals
Life, through me, falls
weeping. Can't you feel the difficulty
of connecting the first line
with a whole life? The hardship of
this life makes life, in another
reality, glide

使我们的返回、困惑、受难
降到最少的次数。那只
诗歌的篮子
最终满满地盛着水
在此生的最后日子里
向上升。水连接水
水拉着水向上
在诗歌的清澈宁静里
为仍旧有许多次生命的人们
在自己的完整的爱中
为他们祝福

Much love turns us, vertiginous, takes
away suffering. The ark of poetry, at last
watertight, rises in the latest
days of this life. Water to
water. Water lifts water
in the clear calm of poetry
In my love's fullness I
bless those who still
have many lives to live

我的家

我的家在午后一个温暖的日子
　　　结满葡萄
我的妻象只红色温柔的小狐狸
把她细细的手
伸入我音乐交错的胸中

窗子的玻璃上趴满蜜蜂
花朵在一个个字里开放
我的妻穿着红色的衣服跑跳着
把朝向阳光的门带得哐哐的响…

我坐在一把古铜色的椅子里
听着远处的庭园里草根吵闹的声音
听一滴水慢慢渗进一块石头
一只鸟，在远远的
我的思想中
　　　　啼叫

My Home

My home brings grapes to harvest
A warm afternoon my
wife, like a tender red fox
reaches her slender hand
into my chest, full of music

The windows are acrawl with bees
Flowers bloom in every word
My wife bustles, dressed in red, bangs the
screendoor in the bright sunshine...

I sit in a bronze chair
listening to roots roar away in the garden
and a drop of water seeping into a rock
A bird, far
off in my thought
                        cries

给圣·琼·佩斯的《棕榈树》

我读着你的字，那些美丽的花朵。我的想象成为巨大的苗圃，你的灵魂出入
那些绿叶子，流淌阳光的水。少女丰腴的手臂插入你的赞叹之中。听见牛群在
每一行空白处鸣叫

那些棕榈树啊！在乡野的情调中把根舒适的展开。每一个壮健的男子吹着横笛，坐在
密集的叶片之间，在曲调的转变中感觉透胸足。一群丰满的愿望唱歌唱浑厚的天空，歌唱阳
圣·琼·佩斯！抬起目光无法到达的地方。于是你拍击父亲纯洁的文字清香的做"时间"的姑娘走
向你目光无法到达的地方！让每一个嚼着你的棕榈树的文字清香的人，在睡意来临前
光中夜静在摸着棕榈树的历史的路
看见通往天堂的路

124

SAINT-JOHN PERSE'S "PALM TREES"

I read your words. Dreams in the afternoon. My thoughts are a greenhouse without a roof
your spirit revisits these leaves which drip sunstruck water. A young girl extends her arm

into the marvelous. The low moan of cows sound in the white space between each line

And these palm trees--even in foreign soil their roots luxuriate
Young men play flutes under dense foliage, their melodies are the deep thoughts of water

rising to the soles of my feet. Saint-John Perse! No shadows beneath these leaves

so your long, thin eyes narrow further: Time is a group of young women strolling in a garden
towards a place you cannot see, but each moment is lovely, well-rounded

So make a rhythm from your father's wishes, chant the honest horizon, chant the silence

of palm trees in sunlight. Let each one who hears taste the fragrance in your words
Before sleep arrives in midday, let paradise shimmer behind the histories of sounds

天堂的通道

我远远看见他
睡眠是一辆
许多座位空着的
窄长车子。我看见我
坐着，前往一个地方
半路上，在左边
我看见他细细地
展开：神秘的赭红
桔黄，几乎使我醒来
天堂就在我的感觉
后面，就差一点点
如果车子开快一点
或者完全停住
也许我会成为
唯一的一个：看见天堂
然后返回。我无法告诉
人们，那条通道怎样
使我在半夜幸福地
醒来。车子开到终点
热带的地方——
我在逐渐醒来时想念
两个我爱的女人

The Passage to Heaven

I see him from a distance. Sleep
is a long narrow train with
many empty seats. I see myself
sitting, traveling somewhere
Along the way, on my left
I see unfold, meticulously, a
mysterious orange and ochre scape. I
almost wake up
Heaven is just back of my
eyes, almost as if—the train moving
just a bit faster or
stopping—I might become
the first person to see heaven
and return. I can't tell you
how that passage
woke me at midnight and made
me happy. The train reaches its
destination in the tropics. I'm
waking slowly and longing for
two women I love

雪迪，1957年6月生于北京。出版中文诗集《梦呓》、《颤栗》；著有诗歌评论集《骰子滚动：中国大陆当代诗歌分析与批评》。

1990年应美国布朗大学邀请，前往该大学任驻校作家、访问学者，至今。出版英文诗集《碎镜里的猫眼》、《地带》、《宽恕》、《普通的一天》、《情景》、《心灵、土地》、《火焰》。作品被译成荷兰文、英文、法文、日文、西班牙文等。

荣获美国 HELLMAN/HAMMETT 奖；ARTEMIS A. JOUKOWSKY 奖；INTERNATIONAL ACADEMY FOR SCHOLARSHIP AND THE ARTS 奖。荣获 DJERASSI，THE SPIRIT & THE LETTER，HEADLANDS CENTER FOR THE ARTS，BUFFALO NATIONAL RIVER，ISLE ROYALE NATIONAL PARK，ROCKY MOUNTAIN NATIONAL PARK，THE MACDOWELL COLONY，ART/OMI INTERNATIONAL ARTISTS' COLONY，BLUE MOUNTAIN CENTER，YADDO 和 THE HERMITAGE 等艺术创作奖。

在美国、欧洲举办过上百次的个人诗歌朗诵、讲演，被邀请参加众多文学节；被邀请参加1999年爱尔兰国际诗歌节；1993、1997、2001年夏天，三次被邀请参加"世界学者、运动员代表大会"。

自到美国后，完成诗集《黑暗里的阶梯》、《家信》、《静心的日子》、《亮处的风景》、《碎镜里的猫眼》、《地带》、《在 MANASOTA KEY 面对大海》；散文集《家园》、《梦的启示》；随笔集《神圣殿堂》。

Xue Di was born in Beijing in 1957. He is the author of three volumes of collected works and one book of criticism on contemporary Chinese poetry in Chinese. In English translation, he has published two full length books, *An Ordinary Day* and *Heart Into Soil*, and three chapbooks, *Forgive*, *Circumstances* and *Flames*. His work has appeared in numerous American journals and anthologies and has been translated into English, French, German, Dutch, Spanish, and Japanese. Since shortly after the Tiananmen Square Massacre in 1989, he has been a fellow in Brown University's Freedom to Write Program in Providence, Rhode Island. Xue Di is a two-time recipient of the Hellman/Hammett Award, sponsored by Human Rights Watch.